Mother Macrina

Mother Macrina

Irma Zaleski

NOVALIS

© 2000 Novalis, Saint Paul University, Ottawa, Canada

Cover: Blair Turner
Layout: Cynthia Roy
Illustrations: Father Ron Cafeo

Business Office:
Novalis
49 Front Street East, 2nd Floor
Toronto, Ontario, Canada
M5E 1B3

Phone: 1-800-387-7164 or (416) 363-3303
Fax: 1-800-204-4140 or (416) 363-9409
E-mail: novalis@interlog.com

Canadian Cataloguing in Publication Data

Zaleski, Irma, 1931–
        Mother Macrina

ISBN 2-89507-042-3

        1. Spiritual life. I. Title.

| BV4832.2.Z35 2000 | 291.4 | C00-900499-8 |

We acknowledge the financial support of the Government of Canada through the Book Publishing Industry Development Program (BPIDP) for our publishing activities.

Printed in Canada.

Contents

Contents, continued...

Foreword

Mother Macrina is an imaginary "desert mother": a contemporary "holy woman" living in some unidentified small town. Although, as far as I know, there is no such person living in the world, I did not invent her. She just seems to have walked into my life one day and, once here, she stayed. She became very much part of my life and of the life of my family and friends. One or another of them would sometimes ask me, "What has Mother Macrina been up to lately? Did she have anything to say?" And quite often she did.

She is, of course, related to some people I had the good fortune to know and whom I mention in the acknowledgments. I hope they will forgive me for "stealing" their lines, but as one of them said, what is "holy tradition" but "pious stealing" from each other? If I am to be identified with anybody in these stories, it must be with Mother Macrina's friends: those who came to ask her questions or seek her advice. Each conversation I have described deals with a problem that, at one point or another, I have had to struggle with myself or that I am struggling with still. This is why these stories proved so excruciatingly difficult to write. From the beginning, I felt convinced that they should be brief, but many times I was close to giving up and felt that it would have been easier to write a whole book on the subject instead. Each time this happened, however, Mother Macrina would, sooner or later, "pop in" and the beginning of an answer would come.

I even found myself *praying* to her one night, which made me wonder if the thing had not gone a little too far! There was, of course, a "real" St. Macrina, the sister of St. Basil the Great who lived in the fourth century. Although I knew nothing of her before this book was begun, who can tell how these things work? In any case, here are the stories in the order, more or less, in which they were written. I hope they may give some readers joy.

Irma Zaleski

Who Was Mother Macrina?

Mother Macrina, after she left the hermitage, came to our town to live. She had a small flat in a house on a quiet street: not very grand, but not a bad place either. It is hard to say what she did all day. When she was asked about it, as she often was, she usually answered that it was not much. "One lives, you know," she would say. "One lives."

As time went on, more and more people came to see what she was about. She did not seem to mind, and even offered them tea. She lived till she was very old, and became quite a celebrity in town. Many people came to ask her for advice; others just wanted to see what a holy woman looked like.

When Mother Macrina died, people were amazed at the crowds that came to her funeral. Three bishops and more than twenty priests were there. They buried her in the old cemetery on the edge of town, overlooking the fields and with a view of hills in the distance, where she still rests. The local newspaper carried the story in detail. Other reporters came too, and asked questions about what she was like and what she had said. People told them all they could think of, some of it true, some, perhaps, not. These stories were later published in a book and, for a while, many visitors came to look at the place where she had lived. Sometimes, one could even see buses from

out of town in front of the house and many cars parked along the street. This annoyed some people, but most only shrugged and said, "Well, it is a small inconvenience, and tourists are good for the town!"

That was a long time ago. Now few visitors still come. The book of stories about her is long out of print, but it might interest some people to have a few of them retold. I hope they are true, although, after all these years, facts are difficult to check. Yet I suppose a holy woman can look after her own reputation, or she might not even care.

Praising God

A young couple with a baby moved into a small house not far from where Mother Macrina lived. The young woman was often seen out in the garden, taking care of the baby, working on the flower beds, hanging out the laundry, or just sitting there on a quiet afternoon with a book. From time to time, as the old nun passed by on her daily walk, she would stop for a few minutes. The two women would play with the baby, admire the roses and chat.

One day, the couple invited Mother Macrina to supper. It turned out that the wife was an excellent cook. When she was putting the baby to bed, the husband and Mother went out into the garden to talk. He had never been very religious, he said, but recently had experienced a wonderful conversion. He had begun to go to church with his wife, read the Bible and had joined a prayer group much given to praising God. He and his wife were very happy together, but he was disappointed that, although she prayed with him every day, when he had asked her to join his prayer group, she only said that "it was not her way." It upset him that she did not seem to want to praise God as much as he did.

Mother Macrina looked at him for a moment and said, "Have you not noticed how gladly your wife looks after the baby and takes care of the house? How much she enjoys working in the garden or cooking your meals? It seems to me that God is very well praised in your home!"

It Will Pass

One day, a famous preacher came to the town to give a retreat. The church was full and everybody was very much moved. One woman found herself so overwhelmed by the preacher's words that she decided to change her whole life. She began to pray a lot and had many wonderful experiences which she felt were a sign of God's special grace. She tried to tell her husband, but he was not impressed and only complained because his dinner was late. She went to talk to her parish priest, but he was not very educated and seemed to miss the point.

She then decided to speak about it with Mother Macrina who, if she were indeed a holy woman as they said, would surely appreciate her new spiritual life. She talked for an hour, but Mother never said a word.

At last, the good woman stopped, a little disconcerted, and asked, "Please, Mother, tell me what you think."

Mother patted her hand kindly and said, "Don't worry about it, my dear; it will soon pass!"

Making Mistakes

Coming out of church one day, Mother Macrina met a young woman who told her that she was faced with a difficult decision but could not make it because she was paralyzed by fear. She was afraid of doing the wrong thing, disappointing or hurting people and, above all, offending God. She had asked her priest, her mother and her friends for advice, but everything they said seemed to make it even more difficult for her to decide.

"Mother," she said, "I am at my wits' end and close to despair. What do you think I should do?"

"It seems to me," said Mother Macrina, "that the last thing you need is more advice. It would be best for you, I think, to go to a place where you can be alone with God and leave all your advisers behind."

"But I am too afraid and confused to make my decision alone. I might make a terrible mistake!" the poor woman exclaimed.

"I know that you are afraid and confused. This is why I suggest you need to be alone with God for a while," Mother replied. "I have learned, you see, that when we are really alone with God, we soon realize that there is nothing to fear and we know what we must do. When we are with God, we can make no mistakes."

"What are you saying, Mother?" she protested. "I know plenty of good people who made awful mistakes."

"If they made them with God," Mother repeated, "they were not mistakes."

Justified Anger

Two friends were having an argument about whether anger was ever justified. They could not agree and so they came to Mother Macrina and asked her what she thought.

"No, anger can never be justified," she replied.

"I told you so!" one of them said.

"But surely you do not mean to say that anger is always a sin?" asked the other. "Was Christ himself not often angry with the Pharisees? Or with those whom he threw out of the temple and whose tables he overturned?"

"So he was," answered Mother Macrina, "but he also died for them. When you are willing to die for those who have hurt you, then you too may be as angry with them as you wish."

Practising Love

A group of young people came to talk to Mother Macrina about how hard they found it to try to live a good life.

"We know," they said, "that we must love God with our whole heart and mind, and our neighbour as ourselves. But we do not understand how this is to be done, for our hearts remain cold and our minds full of our own concerns. How can we learn to love?"

"You must practise it," she told them.

"But Mother, how do we practise love?" they asked.

"By repenting for all that is not love," she replied.

"And what good will that do?"

"When you know how to repent for not loving, you will also learn what it means to love," said Mother Macrina.

How to Become a Saint

Mother Macrina used to tell the following story when people asked her how to become a saint:

"Some time after the death of the great St. Anthony, a young man came to one of his disciples who was still living in the desert. He asked if he might stay with him and learn how to become a saint – like the holy Anthony himself – as quickly as he could. The old Abba did not say a word, but pointed out a corner of his cell where the young man could sleep, and a rock on which he could pray. He lived there for many years, trying to do everything as St. Anthony had done. He prayed and fasted, prostrated himself thousands of times and slept hardly at all. The Abba did not give him any advice, but often, when he looked at the young disciple, he smiled to himself.

"And so years passed. One day, the disciple came to the old monk very distressed. He had had a terrible dream. 'I dreamt,' he said, 'that I had died and gone to heaven. Oh, how happy I was to see St. Anthony himself coming towards me! I ran to him with joy and bowed down at his feet. But he looked at me with surprise and said, "Who is this monkey and what is he doing here?" and went off shouting with laughter like a holy man is not supposed to do! Please, Abba, what does this dream mean, and what am I to do?'

"'My son,' the Abba replied, 'Our holy Father Anthony used to say that, when we die and appear before the judgment seat of God, we shall not be asked if we have been another Anthony, or a Paul, or even the great Mary herself! We shall only be asked if we have been truly ourselves.'

"'But Abba!' cried the disciple, 'why did you not tell me that before?'

"'And if I had,' the Abba replied, 'would you have believed me?'

"And this," said Mother Macrina, "is what you too must learn to believe, if you really want to become a saint."

Stolen Wisdom

A friend once brought her brother to see Mother Macrina. He was a well-known theologian, a university professor and an author of many books. He was not very keen on coming at first, for he did not think highly of holy women and had no patience with fools. But his sister persisted and, once he came, he seemed to enjoy himself and was in no hurry to leave.

His sister later told Mother Macrina that when she asked her brother what he thought of the visit, he replied that Mother seemed to be a very intelligent and well-read woman, but that nothing she had said was in fact new, for it was all taken from the writings of the Fathers of the Church and the saints.

When she heard this, Mother burst out laughing and said, "Your brother is perfectly right, of course. Everything I know, I steal from the saints! But this does not worry me at all, for they themselves stole everything they knew from God."

Reading the Gospel

One year, there was quite a commotion among churchgoers in town. It had been reported that some prominent scholars were meeting to decide which parts of the Gospels were to be believed and which ones to be thrown away. This created great excitement among the experts and much discussion in the popular press. Many sermons were preached on the subject, some warning of dire consequences of such impiety, but others hailing it as the greatest breakthrough in biblical scholarship to date. Some of Mother Macrina's friends were very upset, and could not understand why she did not seem to be much bothered by it all. They talked it over among themselves and decided to tell her how they felt.

"Well," Mother said, "this is not the end of the world. The Gospel is more than the pages it is written on and cannot be destroyed by anything the learned professors may do."

"But Mother," they protested, "what these scholars are doing is surely a terrible sin." "Maybe," she replied, "but that is God's business, not ours."

One of the scholars had a cousin in town and came to visit him one day. Having heard of Mother Macrina, he asked if he could meet her while he was here. His cousin was a little doubtful, for

Mother could be somewhat rude at times, and the professor's ego was not difficult to bruise. But, to his relief, Mother invited them in quite politely and even offered them tea.

While they were chatting about different things, the professor noticed a large book of the Gospels lying open on a wooden stand in a corner of the room. "I see you read the Gospels," he said. "As you may know, I am a specialist in the field. Would you like to ask me some questions? I should be glad to discuss with you anything you wish."

"No, thank you, Professor," Mother replied. "I never study the Gospels and am quite unlearned."

"Oh," said the professor. "How, then, do you read them?"

"Very easily," answered Mother Macrina. "On my knees!"

Be Sorry!

A woman came to tell Mother Macrina about a quarrel she had had with a friend. She explained in detail how it came about, and how difficult her friend had been. She was sorry she got so angry, but still....

Mother listened patiently till the woman ran out of breath. Then she asked her, "Why don't you tell your friend you are sorry and be done with it?"

"But, Mother," the woman exclaimed, "did you not listen to me at all? It wasn't my fault; I explained it to you already!"

"So you did," answered Mother Macrina. "What a strange thing it is that to say one is sorry takes only a moment, but to explain why one should *not* say it takes over an hour!"

How God Treats His Friends

A very pious and good woman complained to Mother Macrina about the treatment she had lately received from God. It seemed to her that ever since she had returned to the practice of her faith and tried to lead a good life, one disaster after another had happened to her. Her husband had lost his job, her daughter had gotten married and moved away, her best friend did not understand her and thought religion was an escape from life, she had quarrelled with her brother, and now even her health was beginning to break down. Truly, it was too much to bear, and she could not understand why God would allow such things to happen to his friends!

"But my dear," said Mother Macrina, "*why not?*"

Ceaseless Repentance

One day, a man came to see Mother Macrina. He wished to discuss with her a sermon on "ceaseless repentance" that he had just heard. He could not understand, he said, why, in this day and age, the Church still had to insist on making him feel guilty for no reason at all. He did not, of course, consider himself perfect or a saint but, on the whole, he believed he was doing fine. He lived a moral life, worked hard, had a happy family and helped his neighbour as much as he could. Surely he had no need to repent every day of his life.

"Yes, I see your problem," said Mother Macrina. "You are a good man and don't have many sins for which to repent. But do not let this worry you, my friend, for it seems you have a few virtues for which you *can* repent."

The man was shocked and looked at her with dismay. "Mother, what are you saying?" he exclaimed. "How can I repent for my virtues or the good I have done? Are we not told to strive to be good and lead blameless lives?"

"Yes, of course," answered Mother Macrina, "but *never* to imagine that we have succeeded."

Victory over Evil

*E*very year, Mother Macrina used to spend a few days in the monastery just outside of town. At the end of her stay, the abbot, who was a good friend of hers, often asked her to meet with his monks for a short talk.

During one of those meetings, she spoke about how victory over evil must be won. When we forgive those who have hurt us, pray for them and wish them well, she said, we turn the evil they have done into good.

"I do not understand this at all," one of the monks objected. "Are you saying that when we forgive an evil man, he immediately turns into a saint?"

"It can happen, you know," Mother Macrina replied. "True forgiveness *may* change a person's heart. We should not count on it, however, for a forgiven enemy is more likely to hate us even more."

"In that case, what do you mean by 'turning evil into good'?" another monk asked. "It sounds a bit like magic to me."

"It is not magic," she said, "but the work of grace. The greatest victory of evil is to lead us into anger and fill us with hate. And the greatest victory *over* evil is when we refuse to hate but repay it with love. This is what Christ did on the cross and what we also are called to do."

"Yes, but what about the evil we have done to *others*? How can we turn *that* into good?"

"We can't," she replied, "but they can. This is why we must beg forgiveness from them and from God."

Finding the True Self

Sometimes the abbot of this monastery would send a monk or a novice to Mother Macrina to learn a thing or two from her. Thus, one day, a serious young monk knocked at her door. "I have read," he said as soon as she opened it, "that, to become a saint, I must be truly myself, but I do not know what this means! Father Abbot said you were old and wise, so please tell me, what is this true self I must be?"

"I haven't got a clue," Mother Macrina replied and quickly shut the door.

The monk was very upset and went back to the monastery to tell Father Abbot what had happened to him. "Dear me," said the abbot, "don't you know yet that you must never ask for wisdom from one who is truly wise? You had better try again."

So the next day, the monk again knocked on Mother's door. "What is it this time?" she asked.

"I want to know how to find my true self," he answered.

"Why didn't you say so yesterday?" said Mother Macrina. "For, though no one can tell you what your true self is – only God knows that – the way to finding it is clear."

"Then please tell me!" exclaimed the young man. "I really must know!"

"There is only one way of finding your true self," Mother told him, "and that is losing your false one." And again she sent him away.

"You seem to be getting somewhere," Father Abbot observed, when the monk reported to him that night. "Go back tomorrow."

"Ah, it is you," Mother Macrina said when she saw him standing again at her door. "You had better come in and tell me what you want to know today."

"But, Mother, *how* do I lose my false self and find my true one?"

"You must die to it *daily*," she replied. "There is no other way!"

Necessary Doubt

A priest once said to Mother Macrina:

"I have been a Christian all my life, and ordained for twenty years. I have studied theology, taught catechetics, preached hundreds of sermons and given retreats. And yet there has not been a day since I became a priest when I did not doubt my faith."

"How could you ever *not* doubt it, unless you were an angel or a fool?" Mother Macrina exclaimed. "How foolish would we be if we imagined that we have *understood* our faith and made it safe from doubt."

"How then," he objected, "can we ever *know* that what we believe is true?"

"I don't think we can," Mother Macrina replied, "but it is this *not-knowing* which brings us to faith. Doubt is not an enemy of faith; it is an enemy of pride. It pushes us *beyond* the limits of what we can know or express. There is no need to be afraid of doubt."

You Cannot Lose Your Faith

*M*other Macrina was getting ready for bed one evening when she heard somebody pounding on her door.

"Who is it?" she called. "Can it not wait till tomorrow?"

"No, not even an hour," a woman's voice replied. "Please let me in!"

"Lord have mercy," sighed Mother Macrina, and went to open the door.

The woman rushed into the room as if the devil himself was on her tail.

"Mother," she cried, "I am losing my faith. I am desperate and do not know what to do."

"Nonsense! You cannot lose your faith," said Mother Macrina, "so calm down and tell me sensibly what the problem is."

"What do you mean, I cannot lose my faith? I am losing it! I cannot believe in anything any longer, not even in God," the woman shouted and burst into tears.

"My dear," Mother Macrina replied, "you are tired out and distraught, but I tell you again, you *cannot* lose your faith! You can forget it, doubt it, or even – God forbid – deny it, but you can never 'lose' it for good."

"But Mother," cried the poor woman, "I know many people who *have* lost their faith."

"People often hold opinions and beliefs that they mistake for faith. These, of course, can be, and sometimes even should be lost. True faith, however, is not a product of imagination or thought but an *inner vision*; a glimpse of the reality of God. Once you have seen it, you can never *not* see it again."

"But I have not had any glimpses or visions," the woman said.

"Oh, yes, you have," Mother insisted, "for if you had not had a glimpse of God, would you be as distraught about 'losing your faith' as you are just now?"

Wait to Be Found

A man complained to Mother Macrina that he felt quite confused and was no longer sure what he believed, or what was right or wrong.

"I seem to have lost my way," he said. "I don't know where to turn, or which way to go."

"Then don't go anywhere," she told him.

"Shall I be lost, then, for the rest of my life?" the man asked. "What kind of advice is that?"

"The best I have to offer," Mother Macrina replied. "When I was a child, I often played in the woods near my grandmother's house. She always used to say that if I was ever lost, I must not run around and try to find my own way out, but stay in one place and wait till I was found. I think this was very good advice."

An Answer to Suffering

A friend of Mother Macrina's had lost his wife and child in a terrible accident. He was overwhelmed by grief and, for many months, could not bear to talk to anybody, or to see even his closest friends. So it was only a year later that he came to visit Mother Macrina. But, as soon as he saw her, he broke down and could not speak.

Mother waited quietly till he was able to tell her a little of what had happened to him and what he was going through. Then, still weeping, he asked, "Why, Mother? Why?"

"I don't know," she said. "*I don't know*! There is no human answer, and how could there be? How could we even begin to understand, or dare to 'explain,' the suffering which you now must bear?"

"Then how can I bear it?" the man cried. "Is there no answer at all?"

Mother Macrina was silent for a moment before she replied:

"Perhaps it is in the mere *suffering* of it, with as much blind faith and trust as has been given to us, that our way to hope lies. Christ has walked this way before us to the end and all we can do is to follow. Perhaps there is no other way."

Be Angry with God

One evening, a young doctor came to see Mother Macrina. He looked very tired and upset.

"Mother," he said, "I cannot bear all the suffering and evil I see or hear about every day. It is just too much for me. I am torn between despair and a dreadful anger with God."

"Then be angry with God; it is much better than to despair," she replied. "If you believe in God enough to be angry with him, you may, one day, learn also to believe in his love, in spite of all the dreadful things that happen in the world. This is, I think, the only 'answer' to the problem of evil we can ever find."

"This does not make it any easier to bear," he said.

"Yes, I know," said Mother Macrina, "but you see, to find an easy way of bearing it is perhaps *not* the most important task God gave us to do."

Saints in Heaven

A man came to see Mother Macrina to talk to her about something that was bothering him a great deal. He had noticed, on a previous visit, several icons of the Mother of God and the saints on the walls of her room and a vigil light burning before them. He said that he had been quite puzzled by this display, because she seemed so intelligent and not naive at all. He had thought this over and decided he should discuss it with her and tell her what he really thought.

"And what *do* you really think?" asked Mother Macrina.

"I see nothing wrong in respecting the saints," he replied, "for they were holy people who led very good lives. But going any further than that seems to me superstitious and contrary to reason."

"I agree," she said. "If you think of the saints merely as 'the dead' who lived in the past, to reverence them and pray to them, as we do, may seem superstitious to you. But the saints are not 'the dead.' They are fully alive before the face of God and always present to us. This is why we bow before them with reverence and pray to them for help."

"This is very interesting," the man said, "but I am afraid it still does not make much sense to me."

"But, you see, my friend," answered Mother Macrina, "the thing that matters most is not what you make of the saints, but what the saints make of you."

God Never Comes Alone

Mother Macrina once met a woman who insisted that she prayed best alone. She felt bored and distracted in church, she said, and believed that if she stayed home by herself, read the Bible, meditated, or even went for a walk, she could experience a much greater intimacy with God.

"It is true," answered Mother Macrina, "that we all need some time every day for solitude and silent prayer in order to grow into a greater awareness of God. It is, however, *impossible* to pray alone."

"How can this be?" the woman protested. "Surely true prayer means being alone with God? Christ himself often prayed alone, and the saints, we are told, searched for solitude in order to pray."

"Whatever they may have searched for," said Mother Macrina, "it certainly was not to be 'alone with God.' They knew very well that, even if they went far into the desert or hid in a cave, they were never alone, for Christ was with them and so were all his friends."

"But how could we bear such constant togetherness?" the woman exclaimed. "It seems like hell to me."

"On the contrary, my dear," Mother Macrina replied. "Hell is the place for those who really think that they are alone."

A Holy Conversation

*F*ather Joseph was an old friend of Mother Macrina's. He lived in a hermitage outside of town, but came to visit her from time to time. They would meet for coffee or a walk in the park. Often, they would sit and talk together for an hour or more. Some of Mother's friends got very curious about what these two "holy people" could still have to say to each other, and so, after one such visit, they decided to ask her about it.

"What were you and Father Joseph talking about all afternoon?" one of them asked. "Was it about God?"

"Well, no," she told him. "Actually, we talked about the restaurants we knew when we were young and compared the menus we liked best."

The man looked surprised and rather scandalized.

"And we thought you were having a holy conversation!" he complained.

"So we were," she replied. "Don't worry, God was enjoying it, too!"

Ask God to Forgive You First

A woman came to Mother Macrina deeply disturbed. She had had a very distressing visit with her sister, she said, and felt at the end of her rope. She and her sister had been close as children but, since they had grown up, their relationship had become very difficult, and they quarrelled every time they met. She realized that she behaved rather badly at times but she was unable to stop herself; she was too hurt.

"I have tried to talk to my sister about this," she explained, "but she refuses to discuss it and tells me just to leave her alone. Sometimes, I feel so angry with her that it makes me afraid. I have even talked to my parish priest about it and asked him for advice."

"Oh," asked Mother Macrina, "and what did he say?"

"He said that I should pray for my sister and try to forgive her, for only forgiveness can heal."

"Wise man," said Mother Macrina. "Did it work?"

"No, it did not! For, unless she changes, how can I forgive my sister and let her think that everything is just fine? This is wrong of me, I know, but, really, what else can I do?"

Mother Macrina looked at her rather severely and said, "You can begin by asking God to forgive you *your* sins!"

Learning to Pray Well

One day a man came from out of town to see Mother Macrina. He told her that, since his early youth, he had longed to pray *well*, but had never managed to find out how this was to be done. He had read many books, listened to many sermons and even taken a course or two, but seemed to make no progress at all. Finally, he decided that he must seek some expert advice.

"I have always believed," he said, "that if one needed help, one went straight to the top, and so I went to see our bishop first. He was, however, just leaving for an important meeting, and sent his secretary to tell me that I should talk to my parish priest. So I did, but he said that he had a big parish to run and had hardly enough time to celebrate the liturgy or listen to his parishioners' sins. So what could he tell me about prayer, for goodness' sake?

"'You need to find somebody who has time to pray,' he told me, 'a kind of holy person, a hermit or perhaps even a nun. I don't think there is anybody like that in this town, but there is a woman in the next one who might help you out. I hear she does not do anything much all day, so I suppose she must know how to pray.'

"And this is why I am here," he concluded.

At this, Mother Macrina started to laugh so hard that the man began to wonder whether she was not a little odd. But, after a while, she stopped laughing and said, "My dear man, it is true that I do not do much all day but, I assure you, this has not taught me how to pray! It has rather convinced me that I may never learn."

The man could not hide his disapproval. "Mother," he protested, "if what you say is true, it is a tragedy, not something to laugh about!"

"You are right," she told him. "There is no greater pain than not knowing how to pray. Yet, we should not let this surprise us or make us despondent, for we are weak human beings and, while still on earth, we cannot pray 'well,' as the angels do. But one day, they will teach us in heaven and then, my friend, *how* we shall pray!"

"And what do we do in the meantime?" he persisted.

"We pray *badly*," Mother Macrina replied, "and repent for not praying well."

Don't Be Anxious

A celebrated psychotherapist once visited Mother Macrina. He was an expert in anxiety, he told her, and had many patients who suffered from that painful condition, which he found difficult to cure. He wanted to talk to her, for he hoped that her long experience with people might be helpful to him in his work.

"My dear doctor," said Mother Macrina, "if I knew a cure for anxiety, I would cure myself of it first of all."

He was quite taken aback by this reply.

"Do you mean to say that you suffer from anxiety yourself?" he asked. "I would not have imagined it likely, judging by all I have heard!"

"I don't know what you have heard, but anxiety seems to me inseparable from the human condition," she replied. "We are mortal beings, placed in circumstances often beyond our control, threatened with disaster and afraid of death. We are unable to forget what happened to us yesterday or know what may happen tomorrow. A human being who is free from anxiety is rare indeed."

"But Mother, you are, I presume, a religious person, a Christian no doubt. Did not Christ command his disciples not to be anxious or 'worry about tomorrow,' but in all things trust in the Providence of God?"

"Yes, but he did not say it was easy or even possible to achieve in this life. Christ's call to us is not, I believe, a command never to *feel* anxious, but rather an indication of *how* we should deal with it when we do."

"And how do you deal with it?"

"By *remembering God*," Mother Macrina replied. "Anxiety might be viewed as a call to seek, again and again, the presence of God – the only 'place' where we can be truly free from all fear."

"But what can you tell those who are not religious? Who do not even believe in God?" the doctor asked her.

"Not much," she replied. "That, it seems to me, is *your* job."

First Things First

A man told Mother Macrina about a friend of his who had become a Buddhist nun. She had spent many years living alone in a cave in the Himalayas before returning recently to the West. She appeared to be a very wise and holy person and many people were beginning to seek her spiritual advice and help.

"What a pity that my friend is not a Christian," he said. "Please, Mother, pray hard for her conversion."

"Why don't you ask her first to pray for mine?" Mother Macrina replied.

One Kind of Prayer

One day a group of students came to talk to Mother Macrina.

"Mother," they asked, "how many kinds of prayer are there, and which is the highest of them all?"

She looked quite annoyed and said, "What kind of foolish question is that? No, don't tell me. I know. You are taking a course on prayer at school."

They admitted rather sheepishly that it was so.

"We have to write a term paper on the main kinds of prayer and the level of spiritual life each of them requires," they explained.

"Lord, have mercy!" sighed Mother Macrina. "How on earth can anybody expect you to have any sense left by the time you are through?"

But, seeing how mystified they were and that they had no idea what she was talking about, she relented and told them to sit down.

"There are not many 'kinds' of prayer, or ways of 'doing' it – only one," she told them. "To pray is to be in God's presence, and nothing else can be called 'prayer' at all."

"Yes, Mother," one of them said, looking clever and quite pleased with himself, "but when we *are* in God's presence, what is it that we must say or do?"

Mother Macrina sighed again, but replied as patiently as she could.

"When you are in God's presence, you can 'do' or 'say' whatever you wish. You can ask for anything you need, repent for your sins, be silent or talk, sing, dance or even stand on your head!" she said and sent them away.

What Flying a Kite Might Teach Us

A priest complained to Mother Macrina that, whatever he said or did, he could not get some people to love God as they should. "They just don't get it," he said, "and I really don't know what else I can do."

"You might try leaving them alone for a while," she replied. Then, she told him this story:

"My old friend, Father Joseph, used to love kites. He would fly them whenever he could. One day he was given a lovely red kite which looked perfect but just would not fly. Although he tried and tried, he could not get it off the ground. So he put it aside and nearly forgot it was there. One morning, however, when he woke up, he saw that it was a glorious day. The sun was shining, the grass was green, and there was a breeze.

"'This is it!' he thought, 'this is the day my red kite will fly!'

"And so it was. He took the kite to a nearby meadow and threw it into the air. It took off at once and flew straight into the sky.

"'Aha!' he said to himself, 'this is how it is between God and each human soul. God knows best when it is the right time to blow.'

"And so," added Mother Macrina, "it might be a good idea to let God do his job!"

The Secret of Repentance

*S*ome friends asked Mother Macrina why she liked to talk about repentance so much.

"You seem to bring it into nearly every conversation," they complained. "We know that we must repent when we have committed a sin. We must ask for forgiveness and try to make amends. But you seem to suggest that we should repent of something all day! Surely God does not want *that* from us?"

"It is not a question of what God wants from us, but of what *we* want from God," said Mother Macrina. "We repent because we long for God's presence and his *unconditional* love. This is what we ask for when we call for mercy."

A young man who had not spoken a word till then turned to her and said, "But how can such love ever be possible for us? How could our hearts bear it and not break? For we are so puny and God is so great! We are so imperfect, full of doubt and fear, and he is so holy, so beautiful and good!"

"Ah," Mother Macrina replied, "if you have learned this already, my friend, you have learned the secret of true repentance and of highest joy."

Resist No Evil

"I have recently attended a lecture on 'non-resistance' which greatly disturbed me," a man told Mother Macrina. "The speaker insisted that no use of force was ever allowed by Christ. But how could this be? How could we live in a world so full of evil and not resist it with all our strength? Should a society not defend itself from an attack or let the evildoer go free? Would this not bring about even more violence and sin?"

"Christ did not address himself to societies or governments," she replied. "The use of force may seem unavoidable at times; there may be no other way. The command of Christ to his *disciples*, however, is clear: *resist no evil*, but love your enemy and forgive him the evil he has done."

"Yes, but Christ was perfect and we are not!" the man protested. "We *cannot* always do as he did or love the way he told us to love. If we tried, we might become discouraged or even fall into despair."

"Each of us has been given only a small task to do," said Mother Macrina. "We must pull out the weeds of resentment, envy or hate from our own hearts, as long as we live. But, because we so often fail, because the weeds spring up again or evil in the world overwhelms us at times and forces us to compromise, we must repent and try again and again. This is our work as long as we live."

❧

A Sinner's Peace

A woman told Mother Macrina that she had lately become acutely aware of how badly she had lived, how many people she had hurt, how much she had sinned. There were things she had done that could not be undone and they were weighing heavily on her mind.

"How can I come to terms with the evil I have done in the past?" she cried.

"I don't think you can," Mother Macrina replied. "Not until you learn to come to terms with the evil you do today and may do tomorrow."

Self-Improvement

A friend told Mother Macrina that she had been feeling very discouraged of late. She had been trying to become a better person and to be easier to live with, but was finding it so hard she was ready to give up the struggle.

"I have gone to counsellors and therapists and have joined a self-help group," she said. "I have attended healing workshops, followed special diets, tried acupuncture and shiatsu massage. I now know a whole lot more about myself than I have ever known – or even wanted to know – but this does not seem to have improved me very much at all. I am still the same miserable self and I doubt I shall ever change."

"You probably won't," Mother agreed. "But then, you are not asked to *improve* your 'miserable self.' You are asked to *lose* it!"

One Sinner to Another

One summer, a young priest came to visit Mother Macrina. "I am disgusted with the state of the Church these days," he announced, "and have a million questions I hope you can answer."

"Why me?" Mother asked. "I am not an expert in the field and can offer no advice. You should see my friend Father Joseph, I think. He will help you."

So the priest went off and was gone a week. On his return, he came to see Mother Macrina again to tell her about what happened during his visit with Father Joseph.

"When I arrived that first day," he said, "Father Joseph greeted me kindly and listened to all I had to say. But then he said, 'These are very important questions you have asked – too important to answer right away. Why don't you go and work in the garden today, and we shall talk tomorrow.'

"I did not like the idea, but then, I thought, 'Why not? One day won't kill me and I might just as well help this nice old fellow out.' And so, all that day, I dug in the garden and sweated in the sun. The next morning, as soon as I got up, I went over to Father Joseph's cabin to have our talk. However, it was not to be.

"'Today is not a good day to talk,' he said. 'There is too much to be done. If you help in the garden again, we shall talk tomorrow.'

"But seeing how disappointed and annoyed I was, he said, 'It seems you may need a little help. So, as you work, repeat these words: *Lord have mercy on me! Lord have mercy on me!* over and over again. You'll soon feel better, you'll see.'

'Oh, come on, Father!' I protested. 'I know I am a sinner, but surely not so great that I need to pray for mercy all day long, especially when I am breaking my back for you!'

"'Okay, then,' he replied, 'you can say this prayer instead: *Lord have mercy on Joseph, the greatest sinner of all!*'"

"And did you?" Mother Macrina asked him.

"I did," he replied, "although, I must tell you, I could barely stop myself from strangling that 'nice old fellow' or hitting him with the spade!"

"Oh, dear!" she said. "Was it as bad as that?"

"Well, it was at first," said the priest, "but, in the end, it did not turn out so bad. On Sunday, after the liturgy, Father Joseph came to me and said, 'Now, fire away! I think I can answer all your questions about the state of the Church today.'

"And could he?" asked Mother Macrina.

"Actually," the priest answered a little sheepishly, "he couldn't. Because by then, you see, I had forgotten every question I had thought I had!"

Two Wise People

*T*here was a group of students of a Tibetan Lama living in town. One year, the Lama came to visit them for a few days. He had heard of Mother Macrina and wanted to meet her. And so, one afternoon, he came to her place for tea.

The two old people talked a little, but mostly they sat smiling at each other and drinking their tea.

The Lama said, "My students think too much. They think and think and won't let their small minds go. That is not so good."

"No, it isn't," Mother Macrina agreed. "But perhaps one day they will realize they cannot think their way to truth."

"That's very good," he said. "We call it 'beginning of enlightenment.'"

"We call it humility," she replied.

The Lama laughed. "And so it is," he said. "So it is!"

They bowed to each other and the Lama left.

Nothing Left

"We are told," a woman said to Mother Macrina, "that we should 'die to self' – that we should deny it, forget it and leave it behind."

"That is right," Mother replied.

"But if I leave my self behind, what shall I be left with?" the woman exclaimed. "Nothing at all!"

"Precisely," said Mother Macrina. "Nothing but God."

An Ordinary Prayer

*M*other Macrina was walking one day when a neighbour saw her and invited her in for a cup of tea. The neighbour had just returned from a visit to a friend, she said, a very pious woman who had a prayer group meeting at her house every week.

"I found this very moving," she told Mother Macrina, "but also distressing to find my own prayer so ordinary and dull in comparison with theirs."

"Well, did you try to pray like they did?"

"Of course I tried," the woman replied, "but it did not seem to work for me at all. I felt very self-conscious and a little unreal."

"So what is your problem?" Mother wanted to know. "It is never wise to force yourself to pray the way other people do or to experience emotions that are not your own."

"But how else can I learn to pray?" the woman asked.

"Only by being yourself," Mother Macrina replied. "I met a wise bishop once who gave me this advice: 'Never say one word to God that you do not really mean.' You might want to think about that for a while." Having said this, she finished her tea and went on her way.

A week later, the woman saw her again and asked her to come in.

"I thought a lot about what you told me the last time," she said, "and was shocked to realize that the only time I *really* mean what I say to God is when I badger him for something I need!"

"And what is wrong with badgering God?" asked Mother Macrina.

"It seems not only ordinary and dull, but selfish and unnecessary, too! Surely God already knows very well what we need?"

"It is true that God knows what we need," Mother replied, "but do *we* really know how much we need God? And how can we learn that unless we begin to pray 'selfishly,' like little children, for everything we need?"

"I think I understand what you are telling me," the woman said with a sigh, "but I would still like to learn to pray as beautifully as my friend does."

"Perhaps you will, one day," said Mother Macrina, "and perhaps one day your friend will learn to pray like you!"

What Is Faith?

A student came to Mother Macrina in great distress.

"Mother," he said, "I don't know what to do! The more I learn about faith the less I know what it is."

"And what do you think faith is?" Mother asked.

"But this is the problem, you see," he replied. "I can't think of anything at all."

"Good!" she said. "That means you are getting somewhere!"

Talking About God

A woman said to Mother Macrina: "I cannot bear any longer all this pious talk about God. We don't even *know* who God is, so why can't we stop talking as if we did?"

"Yes, it does get a little tiresome at times, doesn't it?" Mother replied. "But we are only human and must talk about things that matter to us most, even when we do not know what we really mean. Words are only shadows of the reality we seek, but we must use them, for they are also signs pointing to what lies beyond."

"But I don't want to see shadows or signs," the young woman exclaimed. "I want to see God!"

"My dear," said Mother Macrina, "for that, you must indeed stop talking and *wait.*"

Yo-Yo Advice

A woman came to talk to Mother Macrina about the many painful doubts and questions that filled her mind and would give her no peace.

"Please, Mother, help me if you can," she asked, "or I think I shall go insane."

"When I was a young woman," Mother Macrina told her, "I was often tormented by conflicting ideas and doubts. So one day I went to see my friend Father Joseph and asked for his help.

"I spoke for a long time, but he only sat in his chair and played with a yo-yo, which he always kept on his desk.

'It is okay, my dear,' he told me at one point, 'I am all ears.'

"I went on for a while longer but finally I got very angry. 'For goodness sake, Father,' I shouted, 'put that silly toy away and give me some advice!'

"Father Joseph grinned at me and said, 'I will put away my yo-yo when you put away the one you have in your head.'

"And do you know," said Mother Macrina, "this was the best advice I have ever received!"

A Room Full of Monkeys

A nun told Mother Macrina that for years she had searched for inner silence so that she could truly experience the presence of God. But she struggled in vain to keep her mind quiet and her thoughts still.

"My mind," she complained, "is like a room full of monkeys chattering and jumping around. I seem unable to keep them quiet even for a moment or to chase them out."

"Don't worry too much about what goes on in your mind," Mother Macrina replied. "There is silence *outside*, so vast it cannot be drowned out by any noise your thoughts can produce. Let your monkeys chatter and jump around as much as they wish. Just leave them inside and *you* go out!"

A Common Failure

One day, Mother Macrina met a friend who looked rather depressed.

"What is wrong with you?" she asked.

"What is wrong with me?" her friend exclaimed. "Everything is wrong with me. I have come to realize that I have been a total failure in my spiritual life!"

"So, what else is new?" said Mother Macrina. "Aren't we all?"

A Lesson in Humility

An old friend said once to Mother Macrina: "I have known you a long time and admired you for many things. Lately, however, I have begun to realize that it is your great humility that I admire the most."

Mother Macrina did not seem too pleased with the compliment.

"Thank you very much!" she replied. "I have begun to realize that God gives us enemies to teach us humility, but friends to make us proud of it!"

The Narrow Door

A woman told Mother Macrina that she was more and more convinced that we did not need religion to enter heaven and find God.

"It is rather simple-minded, I think, to imagine that you need somebody to tell you what to believe and how to live," she said. "The door to heaven is in ourselves; all we have to do is to walk through."

"That is true, no doubt," Mother Macrina replied, "but the door is narrow and difficult, perhaps even impossible, to find without somebody pointing out the way. And, if you find it at last, you may be surprised to see how many 'simple-minded' people are already there, waiting for you and cheering you on!"

Father Joseph's Prescription

A man came to tell Mother Macrina that he had gone to see Father Joseph and had asked him what he thought was the best way to find joy in life.

"And what did he say?" asked Mother Macrina.

"He said that the best way to find joy was to accept gladly the cross that God gave us. Do you think this is true?"

"Well, if Father Joseph said it, it must be true!" she replied.

"Then why do most Christians look so miserable?" he asked.

"Perhaps," she said, "because they think they've found another way."

The man came back a few days later and told Mother Macrina that he had thought a lot about what Father Joseph had said, but he still could not understand how his own cross could be his greatest joy.

"I realized," he told her, "that my biggest cross could be my own self!"

"You are right, of course," said Mother Macrina.

"How then," he asked, "can this be my greatest joy? How can I *accept* it? Is it not true that we must 'deny our self,' lose it and leave it behind?"

"It is true that we must lose our *false* self to find out who we really are," she replied, "but we must understand, first of all, how false, indeed, it is: made up of countless illusions and fears. It is these we must 'lose' in order to see our true self hidden behind."

"But how can I lose them? I don't even know what they are!"

"Only as Christ taught us: by love. There is no better way of losing all illusions about ourselves than by trying to love someone else. This is why loving is often so difficult and painful for us: it is our *daily cross.*"

"Well, it hardly seems the best way to find joy," he protested.

"Ah, wait till you have tried it!" said Mother Macrina.

A Wise Fool

"Could God not have given us a more reasonable religion: one that would be possible to understand and to explain?" a young man complained to Mother Macrina. "Do we have to seem so *foolish* to most of our friends?"

"Feeling foolish is good for us," she said.

"What on earth do you mean?" he asked.

"The fear of being despised and thought foolish by others is one of our greatest fears," Mother Macrina replied. "It often makes us deny what we truly believe, or pretend to believe what we know is not true. Unless we learn to overcome this fear, how can we ever be free?"

"But how foolish do we have to be?" asked the young man.

"Very foolish indeed!" she said. "Especially if we think we should be wise."

A Better Choice

"*I* need some direction in my life," a woman told Mother Macrina, "and I have been praying a lot for a word from God to tell me what I must do."

"And did you get one?" she asked.

"No, not yet," the woman replied.

"I am glad to hear it," said Mother Macrina. "Perhaps now you'll try listening to God's silence instead!"

Extreme Advice

"*H*ow do you deal with the fear of death?" a man asked Mother Macrina.

"By dying," she replied.

"Now, Mother, you are making fun of me!" he protested. "Please be serious. I really need to know."

"But I *am* being serious," she said. "The only way of dealing with our fear of death is to let yourself die a few times every day and once at the end."

"This seems a little extreme to me," he said. "Besides, how is this to be done? I have lived all these years and, as you can see, have never died even once. Or, at least, I don't think I have."

"Then you had better begin practising," Mother Macrina replied.

A Waste of Time

A man complained to Mother Macrina that he was thoroughly tired of all the "rote" prayers he had been taught by his parents or at school and all the other set prayers he was expected to pray in church.

"I don't see any point in using other people's words when I am talking to God," he stated. "It is boring and, it seems to me, a great waste of time."

"Well, it may be boring," she answered, "but it is often good for us to use prayers that are not our own, prayers that have been used by many generations of Christians or that are ancient, common prayers of the Church. Besides, even you may find, at times, that your mind is too empty or too distracted to have anything meaningful of your own to say."

"Perhaps, but I still don't see what possible use it might be to force myself to pray in a way I don't feel like praying," he insisted.

"Don't you ever do anything you don't feel like doing?" Mother Macrina asked him.

"Not if I can help it," he replied.

"Then, my friend, you *are* wasting your time!" she said.

A Desert Within

"*I* have suffered from loneliness all my life," a man told Mother Macrina one day. "I had a happy childhood, I love my wife and have many friends, and yet, I often feel totally alone in the world."

"I hope you don't think that you are the only one in the world who feels this way," she replied.

"Oh no," he said. "I have lived long enough to realize that most people suffer from loneliness. But what disturbs me most is that *I* do! I am a religious person, I know that God is always there, so why should I ever feel alone?"

"We may never be able to *feel* that God is there. We may have to keep *believing* it till the day we die."

"What a bleak prospect!" he exclaimed.

"Well, it is a desert," she said. "But it is not so bad. Countless men and women have gone there in their search for God."

"Are you telling me that I must go to a desert to find God?"

"But have you not told me already that you have a desert *within*?" Mother Macrina replied. "If you remain there for a while, who knows what you may find."

How to Heal the World

*A*s Father Joseph was getting old and was often unwell, Mother Macrina was worried about him. So she sometimes asked one of her friends to visit him and find out how he was. After one such visit two seminarians came back to report.

"We thought he was quite well," one of them said, "but it seemed to us that he was getting a little weird."

"What makes you say that?" she asked.

"Well, when we asked him how he was," the seminarian replied, "he said that he was fine but the world might be going to hell."

"And you thought that was weird?" asked Mother Macrina, quite annoyed.

"There is more," answered his friend, trying not to laugh. "When we asked Father Joseph how we could help – the world, I mean – he said that there was a way that he *guaranteed* would work. If we would only say 'God, I love you!' at least a hundred, and even better, a thousand times a day, it would make us holy and heal everyone we met."

"And do you think that you have found a better way?" said Mother Macrina.

Fear of Death

Some friends of Mother Macrina's asked her once if she was afraid of dying.

"Of course I am afraid!" she replied. "Nobody who is in his right mind looks forward to dying or thinks he has it all figured out. We do not know and *cannot* ever know what death is like and what awaits us on the other side. We do not even know whether we shall be allowed in."

"What, then, is faith for?" another friend objected. "How can we say that we believe if we are not certain of what awaits us after death?"

"Faith is not knowledge but a call to trust. We must face our death, as we must face our life, in *blind trust* that God will be there and will love us to the end. Such trust, however, is very difficult, perhaps even impossible, for us, and so we are afraid."

"But is there nothing we can *do* about our fear?"

"Only what we must do every moment of our lives," said Mother Macrina. "Ask for God's mercy and hope for the best!"

An Easy Answer

A young woman said to Mother Macrina, "If yet another person tells me that I must 'deny myself,' 'lose myself' or, even worse, 'hate myself,' I think I shall go mad! What is wrong with being myself? Are we not told to love ourselves as well as our neighbour? Is that not the second most important commandment of God?"

"The self that we must deny or lose is not the self that we truly are, but the illusion of self that we *think* we are," Mother replied.

"But how can we know what is true and what is false in ourselves? What is reality and what is an illusion that we mistake for self?" asked the young woman.

"Oh, that is easy," said Mother Macrina. "Whatever is of love is real; whatever is not of love is an illusion and a mistake."

Who Is God?

A well-known journalist, who considered himself an agnostic and an expert on religion, came to talk to Mother Macrina. He was writing an article on the decline of the belief in God in contemporary thought and thought that a contribution from "the opposite camp" might interest his readers.

"First of all, Mother," he said, "may I ask you this: Do you believe in God?"

"Of course!" she replied.

"Well, then," he continued, "can you tell me this: *Who is God?*"

"I have no idea!" said Mother Macrina.

He was rather disconcerted, for it was the last thing he expected her to say.

"What do you mean you have no idea?" he protested. "How can you claim, then, that you believe in God?"

"A god about whom I could have ideas," she replied, "would certainly not be believable to me or, I suspect, to you."

He did not know what to say to that, so he took his leave. Later, he decided the interview had not been a good idea, and did not mention it in his article.

Prayer for Mercy

*M*other Macrina's friends knew that she had been praying the Jesus Prayer for many years. One of them asked her to explain that ancient way of prayer to him and why she found it so helpful.

"There is really nothing to explain," she told him. "Just repeat silently the words *Lord Jesus Christ, Son of God, have mercy on me, a sinner!* over and over again. That is all there is to it."

"Forgive me, Mother, if I seem rude," he said, "but does this not get tiresome at times? Like a tune that goes round and round in your head and won't ever stop?"

"It does feel like that sometimes, at least at the beginning," she agreed, "but if we persevere, the Prayer soon becomes part of our own inner being – 'it enters the heart' as the saints who prayed it liked to say – and we never again want it to stop."

"But Mother," he persisted, "what is the point of praying like that? What is it supposed to *do*?"

"It does what all Christian prayer is supposed to do," she answered. "It acknowledges that we are weak and imperfect before God, and that his mercy – shown to us in Christ – is our only source of life, of healing and of all the things we need. Such prayer is the foundation of all true prayer and spiritual life, as well as its end."

"But surely you don't mean to say that this one way of praying is the *only* way to bring us to that end?" he asked.

"Of course I don't mean that!" Mother Macrina replied. "I mean that *every* prayer, whatever we ask for and whatever words we may use – or even when we use no words – is a call for mercy. If it is not that, it is not a prayer at all."

"Now, Mother, you have lost me," he said. "I don't see how this can be true."

"We often think of God's mercy as his *pity* for us," she tried to explain, "or his willingness to forgive our sins. But it is so much more than that! God's mercy is the gift of his unconditional *love* for us and a sign of his unchangeable *will*, not only to forgive us 'our trespasses' and give us 'our daily bread,' but, above all, to share his *life* with us and *transform us* into 'other Christs.' When we pray for mercy it is all that for which we pray."

"And the Jesus Prayer can do all this for me?" he asked.

"Not very quickly, if you are like the rest of us sinners," Mother Macrina replied.

Heaven and Hell

*M*other Macrina met a man once who asked her whether she believed in hell.

"It is easy to believe in hell, but much more difficult to believe in heaven," she said.

"Why do you think this is so?" he asked.

"Because we can easily make hell for ourselves," she replied, "but it is impossible to make our own heaven as, indeed, we always keep trying to do!"

"But Mother, I don't mean 'hell' here on earth, through which, I agree, most of us have to go; I mean the one we go to after death, if we have been wicked in life. Can you believe that God sends anybody there?"

"No, I can't," Mother Macrina replied. "I don't believe that God sends anybody either to heaven or to hell. But I have learned that it is possible for us to reject God's love, which is the only 'heaven' there is – in this life or in the next."

"But surely not for ever and ever? Could any human being knowingly do that?"

"My friend, I don't know," Mother replied. "All I know is that I must pray that *I* never do!"

Father Joseph's Best Teachers

During the last few months of his life, Father Joseph spent most of his days sitting by the window of his cabin and looking out at the little bit of the world he could see outside. When his friends came to visit him he would often say,

"See these trees out there? They are my best friends and the best teachers I have ever had."

"Why is that, Father?" his friends would ask.

"Because they are so humble and so beautiful," he would reply. "They bend with every breath of wind but never complain. And they sing such a beautiful love song to God, it can break your heart."

"Beauty, you know," he would add, "is God's greatest gift to us – a glimpse of heaven in the midst of ugliness and evil which, at times, seem to overwhelm the world. Never fail to look for beauty, however ugly things appear to be. That is the true work of love that God gave us to do!"

When Mother Macrina heard this story, she was very moved. "For those of us who knew him, he was such a teacher," she said. "He taught us to see beauty even in ourselves."

We Must Become Heaven

"*H*ow can I get to heaven?" somebody asked Mother Macrina.

"You can't 'get' to heaven," she replied, "you must *become* heaven!"

"I have never heard of such a thing," he said, surprised. "How can we become heaven? This is Greek to me!"

Mother Macrina laughed and said,

"As a matter of fact, it is Greek! The early Fathers called it 'divinisation' – *theosis* in Greek. They meant a change so fundamental, so complete, that, as they expressed it in their fearless faith, *we become god* – we become transformed into another Christ!"

"But how can this be? How can such a transformation take place?" he exclaimed.

"Only through prayer, repentance and love," she replied.

A Glimpse of Glory

A few months before Mother Macrina died, a visitor asked her if there had ever been a time in her life when she did not believe in God.

"No, never!" she told him.

"How is it possible?" he wanted to know. "How could you never have questioned the existence of God in a world that is so often ugly, cruel and sick? How could you never have doubted or rebelled? Never been tempted to walk away?"

"I did not say that I never doubted or rebelled," Mother Macrina replied. "But I was very fortunate, you see. When I was still very young, I was once given a glimpse of the glory of God, shining behind every shadow and pain. After that, where else could I go?"

Two Friends Say Goodbye

An old friend came to see Mother Macrina when she was already very ill. She said that she wanted to tell Mother something she had never told her before.

"We have been friends for a good many years," she said, "but did you ever guess how much I have always envied you?"

"Whatever for?" Mother asked.

"Because I could never find a clear path to God, or was never sure in what I believed," she said, "but you always did."

"Did I?" said Mother Macrina. "That might have been an illusion on your part! But why do you think you did not find a clear path?"

"I don't really know," the woman replied. "I have always loved God, or at least I think I have. But no one form of religious doctrine or practice ever seemed to satisfy me for long. As you know, I tried quite a few but always got bored, and soon began to feel that I was being *unreal* – a liar, a hypocrite and a fool trying to cheat God. So here I am, after all these years, and I still do not know what to believe or what to expect."

"Well, perhaps it is no longer very important to know why we did or did not believe," Mother said. "What matters now to both of us, I think, is to be at peace and to remain 'real' to the very end.

The Word was made flesh, as Christians believe, so that every human path, and every human life, could lead to God those who truly seek him as, I think, we both have tried to do."

"I wish I could be sure that you were right," her friend said.

"Nobody can ever be sure that they are 'right,'" Mother Macrina replied. "Doubt is the cross we all must bear. This is why, at the end, nothing remains for us to do but to trust in God's mercy. Let us pray for this trust for each other, and we shall be all right, you will see!"

They hugged each other then and said goodbye.

Mother Macrina's Last Word

Shortly before Mother Macrina's death, a man sent her a book of so-called life-after-life experiences, thinking it would comfort and encourage her. Mother wrote him a very kind note, thanking him for the trouble he had taken on her behalf. She sent the book back to him, however, saying that, at the moment, she was too busy dying to worry much about what might happen after.

As far as she was concerned, she told him, she only wanted to die as she had tried to live: not asking for answers but in blind trust and love. She was, of course, at times terrified but, with the help of her friends' prayers, she hoped all would be well. She also knew that she was not dying alone, for the saints were with her, cheering her on.

These were the last words Mother Macrina ever wrote. She died a few days later, as quietly and peacefully as she had lived. And those who were with her at the end later said that there was such a smile on her face in death as never was seen in this life!

Acknowledgments

Several of the stories included here are based on or even directly derived from the writings of Mother Maria (Gysi), the foundress of the Orthodox Monastery of the Assumption in Northern England, who died in 1977. These include "How God Treats His Friends," "Ceaseless Repentance," Necessary Doubt," "The Fear of Death," "Resist No Evil," and "Victory over Evil." Mother Maria has had a deep influence on my understanding of the Christian Tradition and thus, much of what I write reflects, I am sure, that influence. I only hope that it does not reflect any misunderstanding of her thought.

Mother Thekla, her successor as abbess, kindly gave me permission to use whatever material I wanted in whatever way I chose. It was she who told me that "Holy Tradition is pious stealing from each other," which I used in writing "Stolen Wisdom." I also owe the idea for "Justified Anger" to her.

Conversations with my old friend Father Emile Briere of Madonna House, whose wisdom and wonderful sense of humour have been an invaluable gift to me over the last thirty years, are directly responsible for quite a few stories. People who know him may not be surprised to find in Father Joseph a faint echo of him. Other people from whom I "stole" some ideas include Father Bob Pelton and Father Tom Talentino, also of Madonna House.

A special word of thanks is due to Mary Marrocco, for reading the manuscript and offering thoughtful comments and encouragement.